The Complete Self-Regulation Workbook for Kids (8-12)

A Workbook about Emotions, Anger Management, Mindfulness, and Self-Regulating Daily Life through CBT Exercises and Fun Activities

By

Mary C. Norris

By reading this text, the reader accepts that the author will not be held liable for any damages, indirectly or directly, experienced due to the use of the information included herein, particularly, but not limited to, omissions, errors, or inaccuracies. As a reader, you are accountable for your decisions, actions, and consequences.

About the Author

Mary C. Norris is a clinical psychologist with a deep understanding of human behavior, and mental illnesses.

She has spent more than 8 years in the field helping tons of teenagers suffering from anxiety, depression, chronic stress, emotional dysregulation, and much more. She also has years-long experience as the parent of a child with severe anxiety. She understands the helplessness of parenting a teen with anxiety and hopes to help parents like these on a broader scale with her professional expertise.

"Parenting Teens with Anxiety" and "The Complete Self-Regulation Workbook for Kids" are two of her famous marvels on parenting kids with troubled psychology and behavior.

Table of contents

Preface

Did you know that human beings start developing self-regulatory skills at three years of age?

If you did not know this before and your child is between 8 - 12, you do not have to worry. This book is for you. Children have a constantly developing brain with fascinating flexibility to learn essential life skills.

It is all too easy to name your child's oppositional, defiant, manipulative, and attention-seeking behavior. However, children's problematic behavior is frequently out of their control. This behavior should be interpreted as a symptom that children cannot manage their strong emotions (e.g., mad, sad, sacred). Their emotions are getting the best of your children's capabilities when they are overwhelmed. That is, they are unable to manage themselves.

The ability to remain calm, manage big emotions, adapt, and respond correctly to our surroundings is known as self-regulation. Self-control is critical because it allows children to succeed in school, with peers, and at home. It makes children feel good and satisfied with themselves and what they can handle.

If a lack of regulating abilities causes children's meltdowns, punishment will not teach them the skills they need to stay calm, manage, and adapt. On the other hand, discipline is more likely to frustrate youngsters, cause emotions of guilt and failure, and escalate challenging behavior. Increased problematic behavior can build a gap in your relationship and quickly spiral into a stress cycle for everyone concerned - but you have the power to intervene. Challenge yourself to remain calm in the face of your child's tantrums or meltdowns. Children tend to reflect on the stress and emotions of the grown-ups in their lives. Remember that youngsters require time and encouragement to develop and exercise self-control.

With a calm and understanding demeanor, let's teach our kids how to manage their emotions and behavior, leading to a healthier brain and body.

Introduction

"You never let me play video games. You always do this. I do not want to eat anything! I hate you!" my 11 years old ragged slamming the door.

30 minutes later, he came dragging his feet with sorry eyes hugging me, realizing what he did was wrong.

Does this sound familiar to you?

Our children often engage in behaviors and have emotional outbursts, which they later realize are unacceptable without any help.

So, the issue is not in their understanding of right or wrong but their ability to manage their emotions, thoughts, and behavior.

Did you know humans have 12,000 to 60,000 thoughts per day?

We know very well that children have developing brains. Imagine how much tricky it must be for children to manage all these thoughts and decide upon which to act and all of this in seconds too. This is why we need to teach our kids self-regulation.

It is easy to mix up self-control and self-regulation. They are related, but not the same. Self-control is primarily a social competency.

Self-regulation, on the other hand, functions similarly to a thermostat. A thermostat turns on or off to maintain a specific temperature, or "set point," in a room. It monitors temperature changes, compares them to the set point, and determines whether the space should be heated or cooled.

We all have a set point for self-regulation. To keep that level of control, we need to:

- Keep track of the changes in our surroundings.

- Examine how we are feeling and how we are reacting.

- Compare it to our set point.

- Make the necessary adjustments to get back to that point.

In simple words, self-regulation is the ability to control your emotions and behavior in response to circumstances. It involves the ability to avoid strong emotional reactions to distressing stimuli, calm down when angry, regulate impulses, maintain focus, adjust to a change in expectations, and deal with dissatisfaction without an outburst. It is a set of abilities that allow youngsters to steer their own behavior toward a goal as they get older, despite the unpredictability of the world and their own emotions.

Self-regulation helps your child's development in learning and getting good grades at school because self-regulation allows your child to sit and listen in the classroom. It helps them make friends because self-regulation enables your child to take turns in games and conversations, share toys, and appropriately express emotions. Moreover, they become more self-reliant because it allows your child to make proper behavior judgments and learn how to act in different situations without relying on you.

Self-regulation is a problem for many children, and this problem grows as they grow. In an emotional circumstance, they act rashly, realizing their mistake after the damage has been done. They cannot concentrate on their goals and tasks. They find their thoughts leading them. Children start to develop self-regulation very young. So parents need to focus on their self-regulatory skills early.

This workbook focuses precisely on that. It is a treasure box of understanding self-regulation and answering your young one's emotional outbursts and immaturity, inability to focus, and negative thinking patterns.

The first chapter reinforces the importance of self-regulation with research, stories, and facts. The following three chapters begin with stories of anger, un-mindfulness, and negative thoughts and provide a practical solution to the issues with worksheets and fun games and activities. The last chapter caters to everyday life with self-regulation worksheets and practices.

Do I have professional knowledge on the subject? Yes.

Do I have personal knowledge on the subject? Yes.

This is why this book can help you. I have more than eight years of experience as a clinical psychologist and have worked with countless parents to help their children regulate and manage their inner selves. I also have a teenager who has been suffering from anxiety for years and needed my help as a parent to learn self-regulation. This workbook combines my professional and personal experiences containing only the most effective practices proven to produce fruitful results.

If you want to check out more on teen anxiety and stress, you can find my "Parenting Teens with Anxiety" book on Amazon. For now, let's see what I have in store for you in this book.

Chapter 1: Armor of Self-Regulation

Our children's bodies grow in size, but their brains develop in complexity. Their brains are not fully mature and have years of growth ahead. We can compare the development of their brains to the construction of a house.

The architectural blueprint might provide a house its shape, but whether the house is made of straw, wood, or brick will significantly impact the final result. Similarly, genetics dictate a child's primary blueprint for brain development, but their life experiences, just like the materials used to build a house, can have a huge impact on the outcome.

Moreover, as it is simpler to influence a house while it is being built than it is to change it later, human brains can learn various skills better or more quickly at an early age in life. That is why you need to focus on teaching your kids self-regulation.

Let's break down the concept of self-regulation.

1.1 The What Part

The marshmallow test, in which a researcher asks a young kid (typically between the ages of 3 and 5) if he would like one or two marshmallows, is probably familiar to most of you. The researcher exits the room after placing the marshmallows in front of him.

The youngster is given a choice before the researcher leaves: "You can eat one marshmallow now or wait until I return, and then you can have both marshmallows."

This is known as 'delay of gratification,' or the ability to repress an impulse (eat that delicious marshmallow) to achieve a different goal– listen to the researcher's authority figure and wait.

Delay of gratification is simply one type of self-control skill, perhaps the most well-known, and it has been connected to a variety of outcomes: children who wait longer are more gregarious, have better grades, and even have higher SAT scores years later. Even their brains showed healthy development patterns.

What is Self-Regulation?

The skill to manage and monitor your energy levels, thoughts, emotions, and behaviors in acceptable ways and promote beneficial outcomes such as well-being, meaningful relationships, and learning are referred to as self-regulation.

It is how we deal with stress, and, as a result, it is the foundation for everything else we do. Self-awareness, efficient sensory filtering, emotional intelligence coping effectively with stress, relating well to others, and maintaining attention are all required to develop this skill.

The Science behind Self-Regulation

Our nervous system regulates our brains in two ways.

The "gas pedal" is the first emergency or quick-response system. Its primary function is to trigger the fight-or-flight response in the body. Consider it like the gas pedal on a car. This system, when activated, allows our bodies to move quickly by increasing heart rate, shutting down digestion, and increasing blood sugar levels for quick energy. When a baby or child becomes overly agitated, this system kicks into high gear, and emotions are at "high speed."

Second, a section of the brain called the "brake" acts as a relaxing or dampening mechanism. This system takes longer to activate, but it reduces our heart rate, improves digestion, and saves energy once it does. This soothing element of our nerve system can counteract the fight-or-flight system's "high speed" effect, and it is essential for controlling our physical processes and mental well-being.

Our bodies run smoothly, and we have emotional control when these systems are balanced. However, when the systems are out of balance, we must use our self-regulation skills to restore them to a healthy state.

It is absolutely no coincidence that the "gas pedal" mechanism develops before birth because the fight-or-flight reaction is so vital for human survival. Every parent understands that babies are perfectly capable of becoming agitated enough to cry to alert parents to their needs or perceived threat.

However, the "brakes" mechanism is not fully established at birth. To make things worse, the "gas pedal" might cause a stress hormone to be released, suppressing the "brake." Self-regulation nourishes and strengthens the "brake" process.

1.2 The Why Part

- Many aspects of a child's day might be affected by self-regulation challenges. Let's have a look at how some of these might seem:

Poor impulse control

- Poor emotional adjustment

- Difficulty focusing on tasks

- Difficulty calming down after something upsetting or exciting

- Difficulty regulating strong emotions such as frustration, anger, and embarrassment

- Difficulty regulating their moods

- Difficulty with social skills or communication skills for their age

- Withdrawn and has trouble interacting with others

- Behave in dangerous ways to themselves or others

- Do not tolerate changes well

- Difficulty with self-soothing

- Challenges with eating, sleeping, sensory processing

Now that we know what lack of self-regulatory skills can devoid your child of, let's discuss what their presence can add to your child's life:

Improved Emotional Intelligence

Emotional intelligence (EI) is the ability to recognize, use, and constructively control one's own emotions in order to reduce stress, sympathize with others, communicate effectively, overcome obstacles, and diffuse conflict.

It is important to be able to express and regulate emotions, but it is also important to understand, interpret, and then respond to others' emotions. Consider a world in which you could not tell when a coworker was upset, or a friend was unhappy. Emotional intelligence is a term used to describe this ability, and some experts believe it is more significant than IQ in terms of overall life success.

One of EI's most important functions is influencing how we respond to difficulties. If your child struggles with learning and thinking, EI can act as a GPS, guiding him around hurdles and toward achievement. It enables him to assess problems, put them into context, and devise strategies for dealing with them.

Here's how it may go if he's having trouble with his arithmetic homework:

- He is aware that he is becoming irritated.

- He contemplates the consequences of yelling or flinging his book to the floor.

- He thinks of a better reaction: he will express his feelings.

- Despite his frustration, he wants to try again because he knows it will help him in the long run.

- He seeks assistance from his mother.

- She pushes him a bit too much, but he recognizes that it is because she genuinely cares about his achievement.

- He asks that he needs to move at a slower pace and would like to do it again on his own.

- He waits until after class the next day to tell his teacher that he is having a problem understanding the lesson.

Improved Self-Reliance

Self-reliance is, indeed, a superpower that can help with anxiety and self-sufficiency in children. They can confidently take care of themselves and take responsibility for their actions. This would pave the way for your children to mature into adults with excellent life skills, like:

- It will boost your child's self-esteem and confidence, as well as their motivation and perseverance in school.

- It instills a sense of importance and belonging in your child, which is critical for forming social bonds and contributing to society.

- It teaches them self-motivation because they are free to discover their own reasons for succeeding.

- It increases their sensitivity to others and self-awareness and teaches them to assist those around them.

- It makes them happy and healthy because they feel accomplished and successful due to their own actions.

- It provides them the confidence that they are competent and capable of looking after themselves, making them more resilient to external pressures.

- Patience, concentration, self-help, cooperation, self-discipline, and self-trust are among the qualities it fosters.

- It enables them to become better decision-makers because they have the freedom to consider a variety of options before deciding on the best one for them.

- It allows them to fully experience life and learn its many valuable lessons.

Improved Social Skills

It is not necessary for children to be social butterflies. Each child will, in fact, have distinct personality traits that influence how they interact with others. On the other hand, positive relationships help most people prosper in life. Socially skilled children and teenagers are more likely to grow confidence in approaching situations and performing activities successfully.

Socializing and being able to get along with others is one of the most crucial abilities for young children to master. While academic skills such as language and math and physical growth and motor skills are generally the focus, social skills assist children in preparing for life.

Almost every element of our lives is influenced by how we socialize and engage with others, whether it's with family, friends, colleagues, classmates, or others. Children's social skills assist them in forming positive relationships, communicating, developing body language, sharing, cooperating, and even playing together.

Improved mental capacity and cognitive ability, and good general mental health are also linked to well-developed social skills.

Improved Self-Control

Self-control influences decision-making directly. A lack of self-control as a child may result in a little too much fun food at the party, spending more time gaming than doing homework, or throwing a few tantrums. In the short term, the consequences of these decisions may appear to be minor. Nobody's world has ever come crashing down because they ate too much cake on a Sunday afternoon. However, the repercussions of poor decisions and a lack of self-control during adolescence can be severe, both in the short and long term.

Self-control-challenged adolescents are more prone to make decisions that limit opportunities and lead to a more detrimental lifestyle. These include decisions about their health (drinking, overeating, smoking, and sleep), money (gambling, choosing play overwork and reckless spending), and behavior (relationships, study, work, addiction, leaving school early, sex, and unplanned pregnancy.)

The brain changes as a result of the experiences it has. It will thrive if it is exposed to positive experiences. It will wire itself accordingly if it is exposed to less nourishing events.

Improved Focus

Think of concentration as a muscle that requires practice on a regular basis to stay in shape. Some children are born "stronger" in this area than others, but all children may acquire tactics and practices that will help them increase their ability to focus and maintain their attention. After all, this is an extremely vital ability for children to learn—school requires pupils to concentrate for extended periods of time, and as they become older, they will have extracurricular activities that require even more concentration.

The majority of children are able to focus on things that are both pleasant and inherently enjoyable. The ones that are more challenging, boring, or simply less fun are the ones that cause them to lose attention. The ability to focus and maintain attention on all tasks is critical because it allows children to learn and progress, which leads to increased self-confidence and self-esteem.

Improved Adaptability

According to a study, adaptability, rather than resilience, is a greater predictor of overall success. The initial response to new experiences, people, and ideas is referred to as adaptability. Adaptability is divided into three categories. Behavioral adaptability refers to the ability to change one's activities or behavior in the face of uncertainty or novelty. Adjusting one's thoughts is a part of cognitive adaptability. Adjusting one's positive and negative emotions is part of emotional flexibility.

Kids who are trained to think flexibly from an early age are better able to cope with changes in their environment and solve problems more efficiently, resulting in a more rounded person at a younger age.

Changes in routines and schedules are more difficult to cope with for children who are less adaptive. They may have tantrums or weep more frequently than their age fellows. They may take a long time to adjust to new hobbies, ideas, or activities. They could feel uneasy around new individuals or even new things in the house. This temperament thrives on routine, which means they are less prone to avoid new situations, limiting their growth.

These were some of the many benefits self-regulation will surely add to your child's life. Let's move ahead with some activities now!

Chapter 2: E for Emotional Well-being

Once a snake entered a carpenter's workshop while the he was gone. The snake was starving and wished to find its prey somewhere inside. It slithered around from one end of the room to the other. Finally, it bumped into an ax and got a bit injured. The snake bit the ax with full force, enraged and vengeful. What may a snake's bite do to the ax's metal? Rather, the snake's mouth began to bleed.

In a fit of rage and hubris, the snake attempted to strangle and kill the metallic ax by wrapping itself around it. The carpenter opened his workshop the next day. He discovered a dead snake coiled around the ax's blades.

The snake did not die because of someone else's fault. It faced horrible consequences solely due to its own rage and resentment. When we are furious, we may attempt to harm others. However, as time passes, we realize that we have harmed ourselves even more. It is not required for us to respond to every situation. We should pause a minute and consider whether the issue is truly worth responding to.

This is a valuable story to tell your kids for understanding and managing their emotions instead of letting their emotions drive them. Let's start with the worksheet and exciting practices.

2.1 STOPP

Teach your kid to STOPP if your child is having trouble regulating his emotions.

STOPP is a technique that can help you deal with overwhelming emotions in the heat of the moment. It combines features of Cognitive Behavioral Therapy (CBT), mindfulness meditation, and Dialectical Behavior Therapy (DBT) to help you confront and manage your emotional response to a tough, problematic, or rage-inducing event.

STOPP is an acronym.

- S stands for "Stop!"

    ➤ Take a pause.

- T is for Take a Deep Breath.

    ➤ Focus on your breaths as you inhale and exhale.

- O is for Observe, the first letter of the Greek alphabet.

    ➤ What are the thoughts that are currently running through your mind?

    ➤ What is the focus of your attention?

    ➤ What are you responding to?

    ➤ What do you feel in your body?

- P is for Pull Back - Take a step back and look at things from a different angle.

    ➤ What does the big picture entail?

    ➤ Can you think of another way to look at this situation?

- Right now, what would a trusted friend say to me?

- Is this a fact or a personal opinion?

- Can you think of a more plausible explanation?

- How critical is this? How important will it be in four or six months?

- P - Put What Works into Practice – Keep Going
  - What is the best solution at this time? For me? For the situation? For others?
  - What am I able to achieve that is consistent with my values?
  - Take action that is both effective and appropriate.

One of the most essential and life-changing abilities a person may have is the ability to stop between an extreme emotional reaction and your subsequent actions.

2.2 Anger Self-Talk

This exercise is focused on helping kids develop a habit of self-talking and rationalizing when angry. Here is an example of how to teach them an angry to calm thought process affecting their behavior:

- **Anger Spiraling Up**

  - **Trigger:** My mother yells at me.

  - **Thoughts:** She does not love me. She always blames me for everything.

> **Feelings:** Anger

Rate the intensity of your anger:

Not at all Angry   Somewhat Angry   Extremely Angry

1 ------ 2 ------ 3 ------ 4 ------- 5 ------- 6 ------- 7 ------- 8 ------- 9 ------- 10

> **Behavior:** I talk back to my mother.

> **Consequence:** No playtime today.

- **Anger Spiraling Down**

   > **Trigger:** My mother yells at me.

   > **Thoughts:** She is just not having a good day. She is just tired.

   > **Feelings:** I feel sorry for her for having to work so much

Rate the intensity of your anger:

Not at all Angry   Somewhat Angry   Extremely Angry

1 ------ 2 ------ 3 ------ 4 ------- 5 ------- 6 ------- 7 ------- 8 ------- 9 ------- 10

   > **Behavior:** I share my feelings with her and empathize with her. I apologize.

   > **Consequence:** No problem.

2.3 Radical Acceptance

Radical Acceptance is a DBT activity that can help your kid cope with overwhelming negative feelings and events. Help your kid use this worksheet to recognize, think about, and comprehend a circumstance or emotion he is having trouble accepting.

Little ones, the idea is to make you realize that you cannot control everything that happens to you. Rather than reacting emotionally, you can recognize your lack of control and choose to behave mindfully. This acceptance might assist you in moving past your distress without attempting to modify or control the situation:

1. What problem or circumstance do you find difficult or painful?

What happened before the current issue arose? How did it happen? What happened next? Who was present? What did you feel in this situation?

2. What part did your actions play in this scenario? What about the actions of others?

a) Describe your actions and behaviors during the experience, and evaluate how they influenced what happened. Keep in mind you have no control over how others behave.

b) How did the actions of others affect the situation? What role did their activities have in the events that occurred?

c) In this situation, what were you able to control? What aspects of your life were you unable to control?

3. Think about and write down your reactions to the situation.

What was your reaction or behavior in response to what happened? What emotional effect did your reactions have on you?

Remember that a response is deliberate, thought-out activity. On the other hand, a reaction occurs when you let your emotions control your actions.

4. What effect did your reaction have on those around you?

Describe how they responded or behaved in response to your reaction.

5. How might you respond differently next time to minimize your reactionary response?

How might you respond rather than react to alleviate your own emotional distress? This space is for you to consider more aware, thoughtful responses in the future.

2.4 What Zone Am I in?

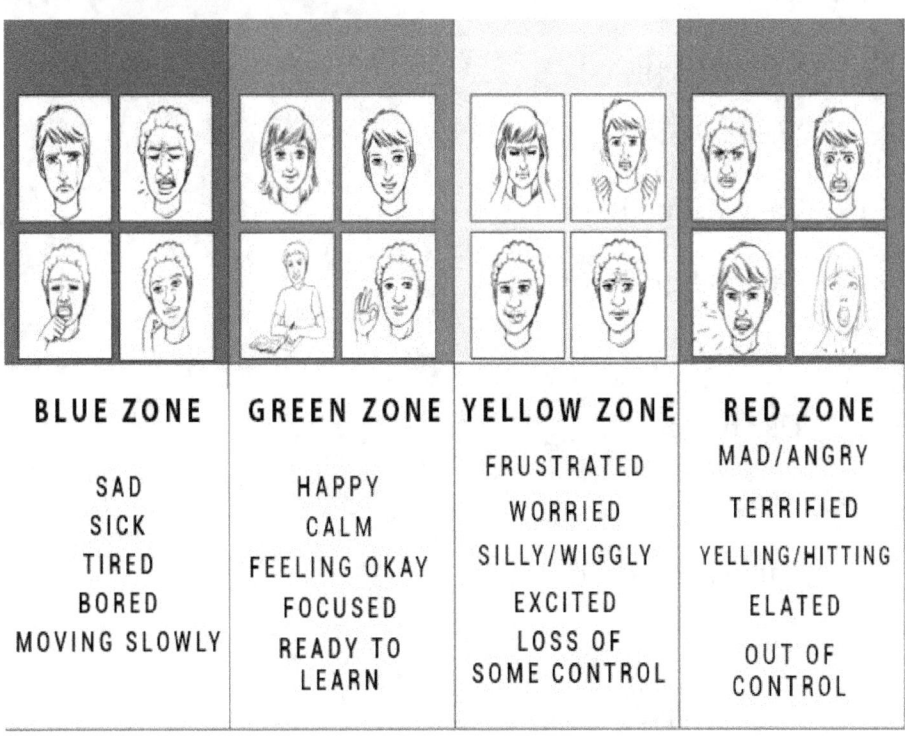

BLUE ZONE	GREEN ZONE	YELLOW ZONE	RED ZONE
SAD	HAPPY	FRUSTRATED	MAD/ANGRY
SICK	CALM	WORRIED	TERRIFIED
TIRED	FEELING OKAY	SILLY/WIGGLY	YELLING/HITTING
BORED	FOCUSED	EXCITED	ELATED
MOVING SLOWLY	READY TO LEARN	LOSS OF SOME CONTROL	OUT OF CONTROL

This illustration employs well-known and simple traffic indicators to assist kids in recognizing their emotions, identifying the "zone" they are in, and considering how to get from any of the other zones to the green zone.

One is least energetic or purposeful in the Rest Area/Blue Zone. The Go/Green Zone (the happy medium) represents pleasant emotions and a balance between extremes. Things get a little tricky in the Slow/Yellow Zone. Finally, the feelings and behaviors in the Stop/Red Zone are the most troublesome.

Once the child has identified their mood and determined which zone they are in, there is a helpful list of suggestions to help them enter or stay in the Go/Green Zone, which includes:

- Count to 10

- Drink water

- Take deep breaths

- Do wall pushups

- Draw

- Use fidgets

- Write

- Talk to an adult

- Self-talk

- Ask to take a break

- Ask to take a walk

- Do stretches

- Volcano breaths

- Lift something heavy

- Think of a calm place

- Ask to eat a snack

2.5 Emotion behind Emotions

A person's behavior is not necessarily a reaction to his current feelings. Other emotions frequently cover emotions. Those feelings are the cause of the immediate emotions. Primary and secondary emotions are the two categories of emotions.

Primary emotions are an individual's basic feelings, whereas secondary emotions develop from primary emotions. The nature of secondary emotions is more complex than that of primary emotions. These are the responses to the most basic emotions. For example, if a person is anxious about an upcoming test, he may feel ashamed of himself. His predominant feeling is worry, while his secondary emotion is humiliation.

It is essential to know the difference between primary and secondary emotions so that you can concentrate on identifying and controlling primary emotions, which are the source of secondary emotions.

Emotion Regulation Worksheet – Emotion Behind Emotions

Objective:

To enable an individual to distinguish between healthy and unhealthy expression of emotions.

Instructions:

Secondary emotions arise from primary emotions. For each of the below mentioned scenarios, identify the primary and secondary emotions.

Scenario	Primary Emotion	Secondary Emotion
Anna lost her favorite pen and got sad when she could not perform well in her test.		
James got stuck in traffic and reached late at the office. He got offended when his friend bumped into him.		
Jenny's friend accused her of lying. On her way back to home, jenny scolded her younger sister for playing a trick on her.		

2.6 Opposite Action

Opposite Action is a practice that can help your kid stop an intense or highly heated feeling in its tracks.

Emotions are frequently associated with certain behavior; such as conflicts following rage or withdrawal following melancholy. We usually think that the relationship is from emotion to behavior rather than the other way around. It is actually possible to trigger a feeling by engaging in an action linked with that emotion.

Instead of doing what you usually do when you are in a bad mood, kids consider doing the complete opposite. If you are irritated, instead of yelling, try talking calmly. Try talking to them instead of withdrawing from your friends if you are upset.

2.7 'Why' rather than 'What'

People often feel uneasy, agitated, and frustrated because they focus on the 'what' rather than the 'why.' They would feel much better if they focused on why someone did something rather than what he did.

Cognitive-behavioral therapy helps people alter their beliefs about why the other person must have done something, said something, or thought something. This will allow kids to take better action and avoid future emotions of shame.

CBT Worksheet for Kids - 'Why' rather than 'What'

Objective:

To enable a kid to focus on "**why**" rather than "**what**."

Instructions:

Often we feel uncomfortable, stressed and frustrated because we focus on "what" rather than "why." If we focus on the reason why an individual did something rather than what he did, we would feel much better.

Behavior I Dislike	Emotion	Reason Behind Behavior	New Emotion

2.8 Nature Play

Like our other senses, the sound is often underused too, and it can heighten awareness and enhance mindfulness. This is especially true when strolling through a park or countryside with family in an unknown setting. Practice these steps with your kids when they need to get away from emotional distress.

- Take a breath and listen.

- What can you hear that is nearby?

- What can you hear from a far distance?

- Which sound is the loudest?

- Which sound is the quietest?

- Try walking without making a sound.

2.9 ACCEPTS

ACCEPTS is a set of skills that can help you tolerate a negative emotion until you can address and resolve the problem. For example, you have exam results coming up, and you are in mental anguish worrying about it, or the school called a meeting with your parents, and you do not know what it is about, you can use ACCEPTS.

Kids, here you go:

- **A for Activities**

  Participate in any healthy activity. Read a book, call a friend, take a walk, or clean your room. Anything that keeps your mind occupied and away from the bad emotion will be beneficial. When you have finished, switch to a different activity.

- **C for Contributing**

  Do something nice for someone else. It will help you in diverting your attention away from the topic at hand. Additionally, helping someone else makes us feel good about ourselves, which can help us cope with stress. Help a friend with a project, help your parents in the kitchen or help your younger sibling in any way.

- **C for Comparison**

  Put your life in context. Was there a time in your life when you have had to deal with more tough issues than you are dealing with now? Perhaps not—perhaps this is the most intense scenario and emotion you have ever encountered. If later is the case, meditate and exercise.

  Is there anyone else who has suffered more than you? Are you safe in your own home while someone else in another part of the world is looking for food and shelter following a natural disaster? The purpose of this exercise is not to exacerbate your existing distress and emotional pain. Instead, put this expertise to work by adding a new perspective to what you are going through right now.

- **E for Emotions**

  You have the ability to elicit the emotion that is the polar opposite of your current distress. If you are feeling stressed, meditate for 15 minutes. Go ahead and Google Image search "adorable pups" if you are feeling down.

- **P for Push Away**

  It is fine to temporarily put something out of your mind if you cannot deal with it right now. Distracting oneself from other tasks, ideas, or mindfulness can help you push away. You can even schedule a time to return to the problem. You may rest assured that it will be taken care of in the meanwhile.

- **Thoughts**

  Replace negative, nervous thoughts with mind-busting exercises like speaking the alphabet backward or doing a Sudoku problem. These distractions can assist you in avoiding self-destructive behavior until you have mastered emotion management.

- **Sensations**

  In times of hardship, use your five senses to self-soothe. Taking a walk and calming music, having a comfortable snack, or watching your favorite show are all examples of self-soothing activities. Whatever appeals to your senses can assist you in coping with the current predicament.

2.10 Feelings Jenga

Feelings Jenga, also known as Therapy Jenga, is a game that helps children to express their emotions and experiences in a non-threatening fashion. You will need a Jenga game for this. Feeling words can be written on the sides of the wood blocks with a permanent marker. Set up the blocks like a typical Jenga game once the feeling words have been written on them.

The setup can be done in two ways. You can either face the words so that you cannot see them or face them out so that you can see the majority of them during the game. If your child is worried about not being able to see the words on the inside, have them help you put them up so that they know what the few hidden words are. There are two variations with which you can play this game:

- One way is to describe the feeling word you pull out before you place it on top. This is a great method to start playing, especially for kids who do not have a strong vocabulary of emotional words.

- Another variation of Feelings Jenga is for the person who draws the block to explain a period or situation in their life when they felt that feeling. You can go deeper by asking them to describe how they felt and how they dealt with that happy or bad emotion.

If the words are visible, it will be simpler for youngsters who are just starting out with this game or who are uncomfortable talking about their feelings to pull feeling words that are easier for them to talk about.

Ultimately, they may get to the point where they feel comfortable taking out blocks even when they cannot see what the word will be as they become more comfortable with the Feelings Jenga game and expressing their emotions. Allow them to set the tone.

If you know your child is too vulnerable to explore specific feelings, it is probably wise to leave certain terms out of the game for the first few times you play.

These are some fun worksheets, exercises, and activities for your young ones to manage their emotions.

Chapter 3: S for State of Mindfulness

There was once a bird that used to fly quite high and tweet all the time. She used to fly from one twig of the tree to another. But that bird had a habit of carrying a bottle with him every day and collecting stones in it, and at the end of the day, he would look at the beautiful stones and feel joyful, but when he saw the ugly stones, he would feel sad.

His bottle was becoming increasingly heavier as he collected the stones daily. After a few days, his wings could not bear the weight well and kept pushing him down. After a while, the situation worsened to where he could not even walk. It reached a point where he lay on the ground, starved to death.

Our thoughts, worries, and memories are like the stones in the bottle. We carry them with us while we go about our day, stuck in the memories or concerns or dreams about the future. Doing all this, we forget to enjoy and be mindful of our present and even end up plating ourselves a bad future.

If your youngster has a habit of staying in the yesterday or tomorrow more than today, the following exercises and worksheets are for him:

3.1 Leaf Observation

Hi, there, young one! What you need for this activity are a leaf and your undivided attention. Follow this:

- Pick up a leaf, place it in your hand for five minutes, and give it your undivided attention.

- Take note of the colors, form, texture, and patterns.

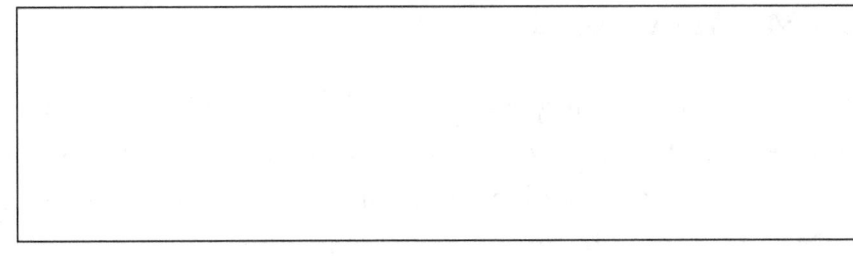

This will pull you into the present moment and match your thoughts with what you are going through right now.

3.2 Thought Observation

This mindfulness exercise is designed to simply increase your awareness of your own thoughts. Guide your child through this exercise:

- To begin, lie down or sit in a comfortable posture and try to relax all of your muscles.

- Concentrate on your breathing first, then move your consciousness to how you feel in your body, and ultimately to your thoughts.

- Recognize what enters your mind, but resist the desire to categorize or criticize it. Consider them as a passing cloud in your mental sky.

- If your mind wanders away from your ideas, identify whatever it was that drew your attention away from your thoughts and gently redirect it back to your thoughts.

3.3 My Anger Read

Acute or chronic anger can be alleviated with mindfulness techniques. As one of our most powerful emotions, anger can be difficult to assess objectively and defuse. Mindfulness can help you create space between a stimulus and an impulsive reaction.

- To begin, sit in a comfortable position with your eyes closed and pay attention to the areas of your body that are in contact with the floor, cushion, or chair.

- Take a few deep breaths, filling your lungs completely and quickly exhaling.

- Consider a recent moment when you were angry, especially one that was minor and resolved quickly. Allow yourself to feel the rage you were feeling at the time.

- Ignore any other feelings associated with this memory, such as shame or sadness.

- Focus on how you are feeling in your body while you are angry. Observe whether any parts of your body are expressing your anger with feelings of cold or warmth, the degree of these emotions and whether they alter as you observe or move across your body.

- Bring compassion to the rage. This can be a challenging step, but keep in mind that anger is a natural human feeling. With compassion and empathy, try to cradle your wrath "like a mother cradling a newborn."

- Say goodbye to your rage. Return your focus to your breath gradually, and stay here for a time until your emotions have decreased or stabilized.

- Consider what you have learned. Pay attention to the sensations that this exercise elicited in your body. Keep an eye on them to see if they altered during the process. Take note of whether or not you used compassion to deal with your anger, and if so, how you went about it. Consider what happened when you gave compassion to your anger.

You can do this exercise as many times as you like. It is best to start with the milder forms of rage and work your way up to the most intense and memorable events.

3.4 The Good Stuff Focus

It is very easy to focus on the bad experience and memories in life. Everyone sees the world through a filter. When the filter is focusing on the bad experiences, the good experiences become invisible to us. This worksheet will help you change your filter to the "good stuff."

10 MINUTES TO RECOGNIZE THE GOOD STUFF

Date ---------

Things, People and Places You Adore

One thing you have worked hard to achieve:

One thing that is going well right now:

Two subjects or pursuits you are passionate about:

Two people you can count on for warm hugs
and kind words:

Three things to look forward to:

3.5 Mindful Half Smile

Half-smile is a simple CBT method that has proven to be effective in reversing negative emotions like melancholy, anxiety, and rage. It is an "outside-in" approach, like many modern CBT treatments, in the sense that it uses actual behavioral tactics to create change in internal states such as thoughts and feelings.

Start to smile with your lips, but stop when you feel a small bit of tightness in your mouth's corners. If someone were to observe you, he or she would probably not notice any changes in your appearance. It is a small, inconspicuous smile. (If you try to maintain a large grin for 10 minutes, nothing happens except your face starts to hurt.) Now put it on for ten minutes straight and note how your mood has changed. The majority of people report an improvement in their overall mood.

When we feel a pleasant emotion, such as joy, we usually smile as a result of that sensation. But, as recent cognitive-behavioral research has repeatedly demonstrated, it also works the other way. You feel good after a few minutes of smiling. When you furrow your brow, you might get angry. You can generate panic by taking short, shallow breaths. Simply put, if you engage in the behavior, the emotion will follow.

Try it the next time your kid needs to change his mood.

3.6 Stress Exploration

The sensation of being tight, overwhelmed, worn out, or fatigued is known as stress. A tiny bit of worry can motivate you, but too much stress can make even simple activities seem impossible. The Stress Exploration worksheet helps you develop mindfulness of their stresses and stress-relieving factors. Daily difficulties, huge life transitions, and life situations can be stressors. Daily uplifts, good coping skills, and protective variables are all things that can help you avoid stress. Help your kid fill in the following worksheet so they can be more mindful of themselves and their surroundings:

Stress Exploration Worksheet

Describe your biggest stressors in each of the following categories.

How does your body experience Stress?

Physically	Emotionally	Behaviorally
Nausea	Crying	Low Libido
Vomiting	Negative Thoughts	Insomnia
Diarrhea	Obsessive Thoughts	Low Appetite

Common Triggers at Home

1. -------------------------------------

2. -------------------------------------

3. -------------------------------------

Common Triggers at School

1. -------------------------------------

2. -------------------------------------

3. -------------------------------------

Common Triggers in the Playground

1. -------------------------------------

2. -------------------------------------

3. -------------------------------------

Coping Skills

1. -------------------------------   4. -----------------------------------

2. -------------------------------   5. -----------------------------------

3. -------------------------------   6. -----------------------------------

3.7 Dragon Fire Breathing

Negative energy and tension are released with Dragon Breathing. It is a terrific activity to do when we are furious or sad or feel like we are about to lose control of ourselves. Practicing dragon breath can be enough to help us relax. The long exhale sets off the parasympathetic nervous system (rest and digest) while also ensuring that we take a deep breath in, which assists us in connecting with and working through emotions. This will be an enjoyable one for kids:

- Sit cross-legged or kneel with your spine long.

- Inhale deeply through your nose.

- Exhale deeply and loudly through your mouth.

- You have the option of sticking your tongue out and widening your eyes and mouth.

- Rep 3-5 times more.

3.8 Blindfolded Fruit Tasting

Sensory play is crucial for young children's development because it strengthens nerve connections in the brain. Focusing attention and cultivating mindfulness is a fantastic technique to alleviate worried or upset emotions when they occur.

Players utilize touch and taste sense to appreciate the moment in this sensory game. The rest of the senses are heightened. This puts the child's focus even more on the present, with the sense of sight temporarily turned off by a blindfold.

You need a blindfold, three to six types of fruit, like berries, melon, grapes, or pineapple, cut up into bite-sized pieces, and a separate dish for each fruit. Here is how it goes:

- Prepare the fruits and divide them into individual bowls.

- Blindfold the player.

- Ask the player to pick up a fruit from the first dish after placing the dishes within reach.

- Allow them to feel and describe the texture of the fruit.

- Now, as they are eating, have them eat the fruit and describe the flavors (do not ask them to identify the fruit yet!)

- Repeat with the remaining fruits.

- Ask the player to name each fruit in order of flavor once all three fruits have been tried — this is a wonderful memory recall spin on the game!

Here are some questions to ask after the game:

- What did you feel you did differently when you were blindfolded than when you normally ate with your eyes open?

- What feelings or flavors did you pick up on?

- Which fruit did you enjoy the most? Why?

3.9 Body Scan Meditation

The body scan is an important mindfulness exercise that is simple to teach to youngsters.

- Ask your young ones to close their eyes and lie down on their backs on a comfy surface.

- Then instruct them to clench every muscle of their body as tightly as possible.

- Tell them to squish their feet and toes, to make fists, and to make their arms and legs as rigid as a rock.

- Allow them to relax for a few minutes after loosening up all of their muscles for a few seconds.

- Encourage them to focus on how their bodies are feeling during the activity.

This simple activity helps children become more aware of their bodies and to learn a way to be mindful of the moment.

3.10 Mindful Word

This practice requires you to pick a word related to mindfulness and use it as an anchor to stay calm, present, and collected. Following are some steps you can help your child practice to bring them back at the moment with the power of words:

- Consider a phrase that has a calming or peaceful connotation. This might be a term like "peace," "peaceful," "love," "snowflake," "hum," "sunlight," or "quiet," among others.

- Make a mental note of the word. Say it out loud slowly and quietly in your head.

- With each inhale and exhalation, repeat your word to yourself. Keep your attention on your word in a kind manner.

- When your mind wanders, bring it back to your word and repeat it slowly and gently while relaxing and breathing.

- Can you keep going for a minute? Can you complete it in 5 minutes?

This will help your kid calm down.

3.11 Appreciation Game

We do not always appreciate the tiny things around us when we are rushing around. We may become trapped in a cycle of not appreciating anything at all!

This mindfulness appreciation practice helps kids to notice and relish the tiny pleasures in life. Give them sustenance for this exercise, such as fruit, drinks, nuts, or another healthy snack. It can also be a regular meal.

Then tell them to take their time eating the dish. Encourage youngsters to notice the form, taste, color, texture, smell, and other features of the food they are eating while they are eating. After that, ask them to elaborate on their experience.

3.12 Mindful Movement

Although children may find it difficult to combine mindfulness and movement, especially when they are learning about mindfulness, the two are not mutually exclusive. By instructing your child to act like a deer this time, the worksheet helps them learn about moving thoughtfully.

We can be mindful when we are still and when on the move. Demonstrate how to walk like a deer. Slowly and methodically, with a purpose in mind, and pay attention to your surroundings. Practice lingering in stillness, as if you are hiding.

Your child will then respond to a series of questions regarding their mindful movement practice:

- When you walk like a deer, how does it feel?

- What is it like to be motionless and camouflaged like a deer?

- Describe a time when you can have a mindful walk.

- Describe a situation in which you could benefit from stillness.

3.13 A Thoughtful Journal

Journaling is a considerably more straightforward way to begin practicing mindfulness than other methods. It can also be a terrific opportunity for kids to practice writing while also recording their favorite experiences and thoughts. Here are more than 30 journaling prompts for your kids to get started:

1. What is your most memorable experience? Make a list of as many details as you can recall.

2. Who is one person who inspires you, and why?

3. Can you think of one thing that shocked you recently?

4. What are three things for which you are grateful?

5. Tell me about a mistake you made recently and what you learned from it.

6. What would you do if you had to do everything you wanted one day?

7. What kind of pet would you go for if you could have any animal (including a supernatural creature like a dragon or unicorn)? What will you name it?

8. What is one thing that helps you when you are worried?

9. What is one objective or task you have set for yourself this week? How are you going to do it?

10. What is one item that always brings a smile to your face?

11. Consider your favorite hobby or pastime. Why do you like it so much?

12. Close your eyes. Focus on what is going on in your surroundings. What are the sounds you are hearing? Make a list of them.

13. What was the oddest thing you have ever learned in school?

14. Have you ever felt compelled to learn a new language? If yes, which one and why?

15. Describe your favorite holiday. Why do you think it is your favorite? What is the happiest memory you have of it?

16. What would you say to your family or friends if you could tell them anything that has been on your mind lately?

17. Would you prefer it to be summer, spring, fall, or winter all of the time? Why?

18. Do you own any animals? What would you say to it if it suddenly became able to speak one morning?

19. Consider someone who makes you feel cherished. How do they demonstrate their love for you?

20. When you are outside, what is your favorite activity to do?

21. Have you taken a vacation recently? What was your favorite part of that visit, and where did you go?

22. Do you have a favorite teacher? What are they like, and what is the most valuable lesson you have learned from them?

23. Pretend you have a time machine. You can go to the future or back in time. What would you do if you could travel anywhere? How do you imagine people of that time would live?

24. Do you remember how you felt on your first day of school? What was your experience like?

25. What are some questions you would like to ask your future self if you had the chance?

26. Which superpower would you select if you could have any? What would you do with it?

27. What is the best method to pass the time on a rainy day?

28. Make a list of one thing you will do today to make the most of it.

29. Pretend you have the ability to shrink to the size of a mouse or grow to the size of a building. What would you do, and why would you do it?

30. Consider a skill you wish you possessed. What is one method you can start putting into practice?

31. Make a list of three things you could do today to support a friend or family member.

These are some exercises and worksheets for your kids to be more aware of themselves, the people around them and their surroundings.

Chapter 4: P for Positive Thoughts

A British shoe firm sent two salesmen to Africa many years ago to evaluate and report on market potential.

The first salesman said, "There is no potential here - no one wears shoes."

The second salesman said, "There is huge potential here – no one wears shoes."

This short story is one of the best illustrations of how a single circumstance may be seen in two ways: negatively or positively. It is all about our attitude about a given situation. Over the years, a great deal of study has shown that the power of positive thinking can have a gigantic impact on how people live their lives and how they feel about themselves. They have more self-esteem, self-confidence, healthier professional and personal lives, are happier, and are less prone to stress-related disorders. On the other hand, the wrath of negative thinking eats you up from inside out. It befriends jealousy, hatred, and hopelessness, closing all doors to happiness and success.

Kids, let's think positively!

4.1 Getting Rid of ANTS

ANTS, or Automatic Negative Thoughts, can direct our conduct without our realizing it and are difficult to regulate. Boosting your mood, health, and overall quality of life is as simple as becoming aware of your ANTS and replacing them with more adaptable, rational thoughts.

ANTS are frequently triggered by certain contextual triggers, such as interactions we have or events that occur in our lives. Help your child list some of their usual triggers in the first column, working their way from left to right through the table; one example is provided to help the little one get started. Write down the ANT that this trigger usually brings to mind in the center column. Try to come up with a more constructive, positive, self-compassionate, and productive thought to place this ANT in the final, right-hand column.

• Triggers	• ANTS	• Adaptive Thoughts
• E.g., I was late for class.	• "I'm a hopeless student and I'm going to fail this class." •	• "If I wake up a bit earlier to get changed and have breakfast, I can fix this issue. I should sleep early at night." •
•	•	•
•	•	•
•	•	•
•	•	•
•	•	•
•	•	•

•	•	•
•	•	•
•	•	•
•	•	•
•	•	•

4.2 Challenging Thoughts

Negativity bias is a psychological principle that states that humans are more vulnerable to negative stimuli than good stimuli and that we can easily become overwhelmed by them. This worksheet will help your child focus on his thinking pattern regarding a particular situation and understand the value of these thoughts:

1. What is the situation at hand?

2. What are you thinking about this situation?

3. How much of this do you believe?

1 ---- 2 ---- 3 ---- 4 ---- 5 ---- 6 ---- 7 ---- 8 ---- 9 ---- 10

4. What does the thought make you feel like? Does it make you furious, sad, anxious or ....?

5. How strong is the feeling?

1 ---- 2 ---- 3 ---- 4 ---- 5 ---- 6 ---- 7 ---- 8 ---- 9 ---- 10

6. Is this a helpful thought? If that is the case, how does the thought help me?

7. Is this a negative thought? If that is the case, how is the thought harmful to me?

8. Is there a way to change your thought so that you do not feel as upset or bothered? How?

9. Are you concentrating on one aspect of the problem rather than all of it when you think about it?

10. If so, what aspect of it do you concentrate on the most?

```


```

11. Are your thoughts about what will happen likely or unlikely?

```


```

12. Do you base your decisions on emotions rather than facts?

```


```

13. Are you exaggerating or underestimating the situation's importance?

```


```

14. How much of my original opinion do I believe now?

```


```

4.3 Turn It around Attitude

Give your young one a piece of paper and instruct them to fold it in thirds and label both sides with the words "school," "friends," "family," "home," "self-image," and "activities." Then, for each category, ask the students what problems they are facing, and instruct them to take these issues and develop a question about how to address them. For example, "How can I get along with my brother?" Then, have your child ask themselves the following questions to change their mindset:

1. How do I feel about this?

2. Do I want to solve this problem, or do I want it to go away?

3. Is it possible that I have been blaming others for this problem?

4. What will happen if I do not fix this problem in the near future? How about in the long run?

5. What tiny steps can I take to help solve this problem?

6. How do I modify my mindset in order to address the problem?

7. What will happen after this issue has been resolved?

This allows children to reframe and offer a solution to the challenges they are experiencing. They will be more likely to use positive thinking when confronted with issues after participating in this exercise.

4.4 My Awe Moments

Recognizing and appreciating small moments of joy and beauty can lead to positive thinking. Laughter, an embrace, a lovely sunset, or the sound of birds singing are examples of these moments.

Starting an Awe Journal with your child is a practical method to build on this ability. You can keep one of your own, and you and your child can talk about it on a monthly or daily basis.

You and your kid will fill in the Awe Journal with sights or events from your daily lives that you find beautiful or special, such as a rainbow, a nice gesture, or even the fragrance of freshly made cookies. Your youngster can capture these memories using drawings, descriptions, poems, and other means.

Although it may appear insignificant, writing about great events can have a significant impact on positive thinking. The Journal of Research in Personality released research that looked at 90 undergraduate students who were divided into two groups. For barely three days, one group wrote about an extraordinarily good event every day. The other group was given the task of writing about a control topic. The first group had still improved moods and fewer illnesses three months later.

Working on the Awe Journal will also educate your kid to look for beauty in unexpected places, which will help her develop a more positive outlook on the world and herself.

4.5 Self Compassion Pause

Ask your child to consider a difficult issue in their life that is stressing him. Following are some instructions for the little one:

Bring the situation to mind and notice if you can physically feel the stress and mental distress.

- Now tell yourself, "This is a painful moment."

  Other alternatives are to say,

  - This hurts.

  - Ouch.

  - This is a sign of stress.

- Now tell yourself that suffering is an inevitable part of life. Other possibilities include:

  - I am not the only one who feels this way.

  - We all face challenges in our lives.

- Put your hands over your chest and feel the warmth and soothing touch of your hands. Say to yourself:

  - I am gentle to myself.

  You can also ask yourself. Is there a phrase that resonates with you in this situation? Such as:

  - I have the compassion for myself that I need

  - I accept and love myself for who I am.

> I forgive myself.

> I am a strong person.

> I am patient.

This exercise will help your child be kinder to himself and avoid self-criticism.

4.6 Float a Boat

Problem-solving is one of the most effective strategies to build self-esteem and nurture a positive attitude. Give your child an open-ended problem to tackle and encourage them to brainstorm solutions. For example,

- Giving your child milk jugs, cardboard, cans, and glass jars from the recycling bin and asking them to create a boat is a fun exercise. All that is required is tape, glue, and twine.

- Allow them to experiment with various ways of putting their boat together.

- Then put their design to the test in a lake or pond.

This is also a terrific group activity.

4.7 Goodness Treasure Chest

You can help your youngster learn to value themselves to counteract the negative bias in their brain through this interesting activity.

Follow the steps below:

- Purchase or construct a tiny wooden treasure chest, or use an empty tissue box.

- Ask the kids to paint and adorn the top of the chest or box with the words "I am."

- Make some coin-sized coins out of thick cards or cardboard that can be written on.

- Then the children should choose "I am" affirmations for each coin and write one on the front side. For instance,

  > I am helpful.

  > I am a good friend.

  > I am kind.

Children can write or create a picture of a real-life example of when they experienced this value on the other side of the coins. This will help them in believing the affirmations. "

For example, "I helped set the table or carried the groceries."

4.8 Wheel of Fortune

This activity will help kids learn to develop a more positive attitude towards their problems and goals. It will help them learn problem-solving skills leaving behind the cycle of negative thoughts. Here we go:

HOW TO DRAW
WHEEL OF FORTUNE

DRAW A WHEEL DIVIDED INTO SEGMENTS

WRITE OUT GOALS IN EACH CATEGORY

COLOR AND DECORATE THE WHEEL

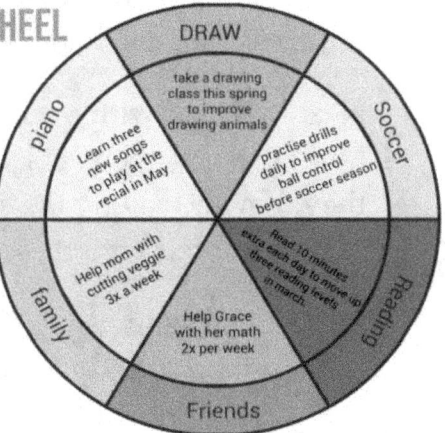

- Help your child withdraw a wheel using segments. Your youngster will put significant categories in their life on each segment, such as family, friends, school, tennis, and so on.

- After that, your youngster will choose one category to concentrate on first. They will write down each goal they wish to achieve in a specific amount of time for this category (this year, for example). For example, if the category is "Tennis," your child might write that they want to practice at least three times per week, improve their forehand, and learn to serve.

- Next, discuss with your child the measures they will take to reach these objectives, as well as any barriers they may face along the road. What will they do if they are confronted with these challenges?

- Allow your youngster to color and embellish the wheel as they choose, and then display it prominently.

- Do something to celebrate when your child achieves their goals in one segment of the wheel, and then repeat the procedure for each successive segment.

Your child will improve in many areas of their life over time as they learn to create and achieve goals.

4.9 Thinking Thoughts

1. This worksheet includes a set of questions to help your kid tackle any undesirable or unhelpful thoughts that are bothering him. Here's a list of questions for your child to answer in their journal.

What facts back up this thought? What evidence does exist that opposes it?

1. What would be the worst-case scenario if this thought were right?

2. Am I overgeneralizing based on previous experience?

3. Is it possible to see things in a positive light?

4. Will this matter in the future? Would it matter in a week or a month? How?

5. How have I dealt with similar situations in the past?

8. Do my thoughts assist me in dealing with this situation? Or are they exacerbating the problem?

9. Do I have any real control over this?

10. What else could be affecting this issue besides myself?

11. Am I thinking in terms of "I must," "I have to," or "I should"? Is it really needed?

12. In this situation, what advice would I give a friend?

4.10 Invent a Recipe

Help your child see mistakes as learning opportunities rather than failures. Instead of lingering on negative ideas, this activity will teach your youngsters problem-solving skills and patience. Let's get started:

- Ask your child to come up with their own pancake recipe to encourage them to make mistakes.
- Make a list of all of the components and their quantities for them to write down. Keep a watch on the procedure to ensure nothing dangerous happens, but do not participate.
- Allow your child to experiment with the recipe, even if he or she adds something strange.
- After you have cooked a test batch of pancakes, ask yourself, "What could you have done differently?"
- Allow your child to make changes to the recipe before attempting it again.

4.11 Gratitude Journal

This worksheet will help your child pick at least three positive things in a day and maintain a positive attitude throughout the week. You can continue these prompts after a week by alternating them:

DAY 1

- Today one good thing that happened to me:

- Something good that I witnessed:

- I had fun today when:

DAY 2

- Something I got done today:

- Something amusing happened today:

- Someone for whom I was grateful today:

DAY 3

- Something for which I was grateful today:

- I smiled today when:

- There is something about today that I will never forget:

DAY 4

- Today I had one positive thing happen to me:

- Today was special because:

- I felt happy with myself today because:

DAY 5

- Today, something interesting happened:

- Someone for whom I was grateful today:

- I had a good time today when:

DAY 6

- There is something about today that I will never forget:

- Something amusing happened today:

- Today's highlight for me was:

DAY 7

- Something that made me happy today:

- Something admirable I witnessed today:

- Something I accomplished exceptionally well today:

4.12 Three Chair Work

This worksheet is a more elaborate exercise and your child will need your help practice it. You are going to need three chairs. These are the instructions for the kids:

Let's pretend you want to work on the issue of being "needy" for the sake of demonstration. The part of you that is viewed as needy will sit in one chair, the critic in another, and the sympathetic observer in the third chair.

- Start by taking a seat in the critic's chair. Now be brutally honest with yourself. "I despise how dependent you are," For example, "You make me seem weak!"

- While practicing this (and the remainder of the practice), pay attention to your emotions, posture, voice tone, bodily sensations, and so on.

- Now sit in the chair of the criticized, and give voice to the parts of yourself that have been criticized. "I am so badly upset that you would say I humiliate you," for example. "You do not care about me."

Repeat this process so you can have a good understanding of how each side thinks and feels.

- It is time to take the third chair, that of the wise and loving entity who has been listening this conversation.

- Relax your body on this chair, rely on your profound understanding and kindness, and speak sweetly to both the criticizer and the critiqued in turn.

- Tell the critic, for example, "I know you are anxious." You want to toughen me up so that I do not get rejected."

- "I cannot imagine how difficult it must be for you to be considered needy for wanting what we all need: affection and attention," say to the criticized.

After your child has completed the task, ask them to share how they felt in different chairs.

These are some worksheets and exercises for cultivating a healthy, positive attitude in your child.

Chapter 5: Balance in Everyday Life

A philosophy professor entered into his class. He brought a few things and placed them on the table. He picked a large transparent empty jar and proceeded to fill it with quite massive stones as soon as the class began. The professor then asked the students, "Is the jar full?" They agreed that it was.

Now the professor took a box of small pebbles, put them into the jar, and shook it to fill the gaps between the stones with pebbles. "Is the jar full?" he inquired once again. They all agreed that it was.

This time, the professor dumped a bucket of sand into the jar, filling it to the brim.

"Now," the professor explained, "I want you to see that this jar is similar to your life — the stones represent the most important things in your life, your values, your family, morals, and health." This means that even if the pebbles and sand were to disappear, the jar would remain full, and your life would still be meaningful.

Stones represent things like your home, car, and job. However, sand represents the insignificant. These things come and go, and they are not always necessary for your general well-being.

The sand in your life indicates the remaining filler stuff and material belongings. This could also include engaging in activities that waste your time or lingering over meaningless feelings and experiences.

If you fill this jar with sand first, there will be no room for pebbles or stones. Devote your energy to the things and experiences that matter the most in life — spend quality time with your family, maintain good health, and do not forget to grow spiritually – be kind, honest, sensitive, and helpful. These are the things that matter the most. They should be at the top of your priority list. The remainder is nothing but sand.

Little ones, you should remember fixating on minor issues, unnecessary worry about the future, turning a blind eye to the good in life, and not contributing to the purposeful events in life is you filling your jar with sand.

Let's go over some worksheets and exercises for helping kids have meaningful days that contribute to a meaningful life.

5.1 Tucker Turtle

Here goes a story:

Tucker Turtle was one of the best turtles you would ever meet. He enjoyed playing with his classmates at Wet Lake School. However, Tucker was prone to become enraged when certain events occurred. Tucker used to hit, kick, or yell at his buddies when he was angry. They became angry or upset when he hit, kicked, or yelled at his companions. When Tucker became angry, he then had a new technique to "think like a turtle."

He can stop and keep his hands, legs, and shouting to himself! He can hide inside his shell to calm down and take three long breaths. Tucker can then come up with a solution or a way to improve it. Tucker's buddies are pleased when he behaves himself and plays well.

Step 1

Recognize that you are angry

Step 2

Stop over thinking

Step 3

Go into shell and take three deep breathes and calm, stop coping thoughts

Step 4

Turtle Thinking Technique

Come out with a solution

Read the Tucker Turtle story to kids and encourage them to "think like a turtle" to regulate their emotions and calm down, like this:

- Acknowledge how you are feeling.

- Think the word "stop."

- Tuck yourself inside your "shell" and take three deep breaths.

- When you are calm, come out with a "solution."

5.2 F.E.E.L

This simple but thoughtful exercise aims to help kids solve emotional problems.

- **Focus on your feelings**

  Ask yourself:

  - ➢ What went wrong?

  - ➢ How did it affect you?

  This includes validating the feelings of the child by saying things like:

  - ➢ I completely get how you are feeling.

  - ➢ I am aware that you are angry or sad.

  - ➢ It is fine to be scared.

- **Evaluate the situation and all of the possible solutions**

  Ask yourself:

- Where did it go wrong?

- What can you do to improve it?

- What is the best way you can tackle the problem?

- What would happen if you went ahead and solved it?

- **Enact the best possible solution**

  Ask yourself:

  - How will you implement the solution?

  - When will you fix the problem with this solution?

  - How effective was the solution?

- **Learn from the experience**

  - What would you do differently next time?

  - What did you learn from the experience as a whole?

5.3 Interpersonal Skills Acronym

DBT can help children teach three important interpersonal success abilities, which are outlined in this worksheet:

1. Effectiveness in terms of goals

2. Effectiveness in terms of relationships

3. Effectiveness in terms of self-respect

Objective Effectiveness with (D.E.A.R.M.A.N.)

D.E.A.R.M.A.N. is a DBT acronym for Objective Effectiveness skills that assist you in achieving your purpose or objective in a conversation. It stands for Describe, Express, Assert, Reinforce, Mindful, Appear, and Negotiate.

- **Describe**

    Use simple, clear phrases to describe what you want.

    Do not say, "Please do not do that, Rebeca."

    Say something like, "Stop punching me, Rebeca. You are hurting me."

- **Express**

    Allow others to understand how you feel about a situation by expressing your emotions effectively.

    Expect others not to be able to read your mind.

    Use the phrase "I feel ---- because ----."

- **Assert**

    Do not equivocate—say what you need to say; do not say, "Oh, well, I am not sure if I will be able to play with you today."

    Say, "I would not be able to play with you today because I have a lot of homework due."

- **Reinforce**

    Reward those who respond well, and emphasize why the reaction was positive.

    A simple smile and a "thank you" can be enough.

- **Mindful**

  It is easy to become diverted into destructive disputes and lose focus if you do not remember the goal of the interaction.

- **Appear**

  Make a confident impression by paying attention to your posture, eye contact, tone, and body language.

- **Negotiate**

  Nobody can always get all they want out of their interactions; be willing to compromise; and say things like, "If you put away our toys, I will put away our books."

Relationship Effectiveness with (G.I.V.E.)

Relationship Effectiveness skills are abbreviated as G.I.V.E. in DBT. These aid in developing and maintaining interpersonal connections, which include both giving and receiving.

G.I.V.E. stands for Gentle, Interested, Validate, and Easy.

- **Gentle**

  Accept the occasional "no" for your demands and do not attack, threaten, or exhibit judgment throughout your conversations.

- **Interest**

  Show that you care by giving attention to the other person and not interrupting them.

- **Validate**

  Understand their feelings, recognize when your requests are demanding, and respect their perspectives; be overtly validating to the other person's thoughts and feelings.

- **Easy**

  Maintain a relaxed demeanor. Try to smile and act upbeat.

Self-Respect Effectiveness with (F.A.S.T.)

The acronym F.A.S.T. from DBT Interpersonal Effectiveness will help you maintain self-respect in relationships. Self-Respect Effectiveness is defined as being aware of one's own views, wants, and values while maintaining healthy interpersonal interactions.

FAST stands for Fair, Apologies, Sticking to Values, and Truthful.

- **Fair**

  Do not just be fair to others; be fair to yourself as well.

- **Apologies**

  If you make a request, have an opinion, or disagree, do not apologize until it is absolutely necessary.

- **Stick to Values**

  Stand up for what you actually want and believe in rather than compromising your beliefs to be liked or acquire what you want.

- **Truthful**

  Exaggeration, seeming helpless (as a sort of manipulation), and blatant lies are all examples of dishonesty.

Kids, when you are in a scenario where you are having trouble sticking to your standards, this handout may come in handy. The brief reminder and helpful recommendations can help you get back on track.

5.4 I'm Great Because

This worksheet will help your kids recognize their strengths and have a positive outlook on life.

- I like who I am because:

| |
| |

- I feel good about my:

| |
| |

- I am super at:

| |
| |

- My friends think I have an awesome:

| |
| |

- I mean a lot to:

- I think I am a pretty good:

- Others reckon I am a great:

- Something I really enjoy is:

- I really admire myself for:

- My future goals are:

- I know I can achieve them because I am:

- Others often praise my:

- I am naturally gifted at:

- It makes me feel good when I:

- Something that makes me laugh is:

- I have succeeded before at...

- The characteristics I am proudest of in myself are:

  _____

- I am at peace when:

  _____

- My greatest talent is:

  _____

5.5 The Mindful Jar

This practice can educate kids on how intense emotions can take hold and find serenity when they feel overwhelmed by them.

To begin, fill a transparent jar (such as a Mason jar) almost to the top with water. After that, fill the jar with a large spoonful of glitter glue or glue and dry glitter. To make the glitter whirl, replace the lid on the jar and shake it.

Finally, utilize or take inspiration from the following script to create your own mini-lesson:

"Imagine that the glitter represents your worried, angry, or upset thoughts. Notice how they move, making it difficult to see everything clearly? That is why, when you are upset, it is so easy to make rash decisions because you are not thinking clearly. Do not worry. This is normal and happens to everyone (yep, grownups too.)

[Place the jar in front of them now.]

Now see what happens if you remain calm for a few moments. Keep an eye on the glitter. Notice how the glitter settles and the water clears. Your mind works just like that. After a short period of stillness, your mind begins to settle and calm down, and you begin to see things more clearly. When we are going through this relaxing process, taking deep breaths can help us settle down when we are feeling a lot of emotions."

This activity teaches children about how emotions can cloud their judgment and allows them to practice mindfulness by paying attention to the swirling glitter in the jar.

Try having the youngsters concentrate on one emotion at a time, such as rage, and talk about how the shaken vs. settled glitter represents that emotion.

5.6 Exploring Action Tendencies

This worksheet might assist you in increasing your child's awareness of action tendencies that arise from both good and negative emotions. The activity will assist you in guiding your child through two key steps.

Help your child identify how they respond to their emotions with a guided meditation. In a nutshell, you will:

- Ask the little one to close their eyes and think about a time when they had to deal with difficult emotions. A dispute with a loved one is one example.

- Encourage them to visualize and relive the traumatic situation as much as possible. What happened to them? Who were they hanging around with?

- Ask them to write down the strongest emotion or feeling that occurred from the experience and try to locate it in their body if feasible. They should be able to label it ideally.

- Assist them in discovering their natural reactions to the feeling. What do they want to do right now? It is important to note that this is not about how they reacted but rather what they wish to do now as they reflect on the event.

The next part guides your client through a guided meditation similar to the previous part, but this time they will focus on action inclinations associated with good emotion. This allows you and your child to compare and contrast the two – what was distinctive about them? What did each of them observe about the other?

This Exploring Action Tendencies activity can assist your child in connecting the dots between a galvanizing event and their reaction to it.

5.7 Safari Walk

The Safari activity is an excellent approach to teach mindfulness to children. This activity transforms a routine walk into a thrilling new adventure.

Tell the young ones that they are going on a safari and that their mission is to see as many birds, bugs, creepy-crawlies, and other animals as possible. Anything that crawls, walks, flies, or swims should require their attention, and they will need to use all of their senses to find it, especially the small ones.

5.8 Passengers on the Bus

Remind your kids to think of this metaphor whenever they feel their emotions are overwhelming. The Passengers on the Bus metaphor describes how our internal experiences appear to drive our lives. The metaphor can be used to show the possibilities of a life in which such events are accepted and sit in mind like passengers on a bus, rather than determining decisions.

You are a bus driver, the bus is your mind, and passengers represent your thoughts. While you are driving, some passengers sit quietly while others make critical and distracting remarks or shout directions.

You have the same freedom to choose how you react to passengers as you do to critical thoughts. Allow those passengers to shout and converse loudly while maintaining your attention on the journey to your goal.

5.9 Best Possible Future

According to one study, visualizing and writing about your best-case scenario enhances happy emotions. Remind your little ones to set aside 15 minutes to write about what their best possible future would look like. Rather than focusing on what might go wrong, they should consider what might go right.

This activity can assist them in developing a more optimistic mindset.

5.10 Emotion Expression

Emotions can be expressed in many ways. Words, tone of voice, bodily movements, gestures, body position, facial expression, and so on can all be used to express emotions. Each emotion has distinct traits, and its manifestation differs from that of other emotions.

When a person feels angry, he yells, moves his hands, tosses objects, and so on, whereas when he is scared, his eye movement increases, he shudders, and so on.

Emotional expression can be healthy or unhealthy.

Banging doors, shouting, and injuring oneself are examples of unhealthy emotional expression, whereas good emotional expression involves communicating assertively, remaining calm, and focusing on the positive.

Emotion Regulation Worksheet – Expression of Emotions

Objective:

To enable an individual to distinguish between healthy and unhealthy expression of emotions.

Instructions:

Recall your past events in which you experienced intense emotions. Write down an example of healthy and unhealthy expression of your emotion for each situation. Also write the outcomes for each type of expression to make it easier for you to choose the best way of expressing emotions.

Event	Emotion	Healthy Expression of Emotion	Consequences	Unhealthy Expression of Emotion	Consequences

5.11 Lub-Dub Heartbeat

The heartbeat exercise is a great grounding activity because it allows your child to focus on their body's feelings. If your child is nervous or anxious, this practice is a great way to help them relax.

For example, if your kid is working on a school project and is becoming upset or stuck, you might gently refocus them by asking them to STOP and take a break.

Have your youngster stand up and hop up and down for one minute or do jumping jacks. Have them place their palm on their hearts at the end of the minute and pay attention to how their heartbeat and breathing feel.

Redirecting the focus to the physical body is a good approach to do so. Your child will have renewed motivation to accomplish the task at hand as a result of this new rush of energy.

These are some activities and exercises to include in your child's daily life for teaching them self-regulation.

Conclusion

Learning to control our actions and emotions is a skill that takes time to master. We are exposed to scenarios that test and refine our ability to manage our emotions and feelings in tough situations from a young age.

Self-regulation in children might take the form of learning to respond appropriately to disappointment rather than throwing a tantrum or asking for help rather than having a breakdown when anxious.

These examples demonstrate the importance of self-control abilities. Self-regulation is the process of controlling one's thoughts and feelings in order to take goal-oriented behaviors.

When a child's self-regulation abilities are working, he or she can identify the source of the impulse, lower its severity, and maybe know how to prevent acting on it. In a broader sense, self-regulation abilities are what allow children to exercise self-control.

Knowing how children acquire these skills aids parents in teaching and reinforcing them at home. Self-regulation, which includes executive functions as well as social and emotional control abilities, has been shown to make a significant impact on school readiness and early school accomplishment, according to research. Furthermore, because their brain and body can regulate and not respond as much, they will be more connected, better and autonomous problem-solver, and happier.

Providing your child with a secure and supportive environment to acquire and practice self-regulation skills is critical to their long-term success. This is especially true if your young one has sensory overload or executive function problems.

One of your responsibilities as a parent is to assist your child in developing self-awareness and providing feedback so that they can learn new strategies to manage their emotions.

This book focuses on providing effective and fun worksheets, exercises, and games focused on teaching kids self-regulation. The first chapter is focused on the concept of self-regulation and the science behind it. Moving on, we discuss the challenges of lack of self-regulation. Lastly, the book explains the benefits of self-regulation for kids, e.g., improved emotional intelligence, self-reliance, social skills, self-control, focus, and adaptability.

The next four chapters are devoted to practical activities. The second chapter specifically focuses on emotional wellbeing. It includes exercises and worksheets like STOPP, anger self-talk, radical acceptance, emotions behind the emotion, ACCEPTS, and more.

The third chapter specifically focuses on mindfulness. It includes exercises and worksheets like thought observation, my anger read, mindful half-smile, dragon fire breathing, body scan meditation, thoughtful journal, and more.

The fourth chapter specifically focuses on positive thinking. It includes exercises and worksheets like getting rid of ANTS, turn it around attitude, self-compassion pause, goodness treasure chest, wheel of fortune, three chair work, gratitude journal, and more.

The fourth chapter specifically focuses on balance in everyday life. It includes exercises and worksheets like tucker turtle, interpersonal skills acronym, the mindful jar, safari walk, emotion expression, lub-dub heartbeat, and more.

I hope this book helped your child overcome his self-regulatory issues and develop a healthier personality. If you have found this book helpful in any way, please leave a review on Amazon and also check my book "Parenting Teens with Anxiety."